DARK

JAY WALKER

The Dark
Copyright © 2020 Jay Walker
Produced and printed
by Stillwater River Publications.
All rights reserved. Written and produced in the
United States of America. This book may not be reproduced
or sold in any form without the expressed, written
permission of the author and publisher.
Visit our website at
www.StillwaterPress.com
for more information.
First Stillwater River Publications Edition
Paperback ISBN: 978-1-952521-66-9

1 2 3 4 5 6 7 8 9 10
Written by Jay Walker
Published by Stillwater River Publications,
Pawtucket, RI, USA.

*The views and opinions expressed in this book
are solely those of the author
and do not necessarily reflect the
views and opinions of the publisher.*

Table of Contents

A Note from the Author   7
I Used To   9
The Dark   10
Broken Kingdom   14
Only Pieces   15
After .CS.   17
Jason 2000   18
This Bone   21
"Victim" Shirt   22
Don't   24
It'd Be Nicer   25
Fallout   27
Lake Inspiration   28
The Thing about Assholes   31
South of the Border   34
Silence   36
How I Could've Loved You   38
All I Can Write About   40
The Ring
     I: Passing Through   42
     II: At First   45
     III: Part of Me   46
     IV: Giant   47
     V: Promises   48
     VI: Through Again (or The Source)   50
     VII: Out of Symbolism   53
     VIII: The Mask   55
Gina Lee   57
Fragments   59
This Is Alone   61
Four-Letter Word   62
I, Picasso   64
Like Forever   65
Fueling the Fire   67
Against My Nature   69
Forgetting   71
How Do You Do It?   74
Lady Winter (or Here & Gone)   76

Your Act & My Stage   78
Splinters   80
Wildfire   81
Fall   83
A Shakespearean Tragedy   84
Memory Breeze through a Wind Chime Heart   86
Assorted Haiku, Senryu, & Tanka, Continued   88
A Mountain that Moved (or Fear's Bitch)   92
The Ground of Us   94
America, Noun   96
About the Author   98

To Faye & all who bring out the light in me.

A Note from the Author

  This may be career suicide, putting out this book. As the title suggests, it's very dark. I don't imagine that one would finish this book with a sense of hope for the future. However, I'm putting out the book, anyway. Why? Because my last book, *Flower*, had some happy, hopeful poetry in it, especially the title piece at the end. You see, I wrote that poem and compiled that book, then spent a number of months pitching that book from my home in New England all the way to Austin, Texas. I thought (and still think) that *Flower* is my opus, my great piece, my reason for being. Its message is so meaningful, that I feel the need to expose as many people to it as possible. That's why I pressed so hard to get it out there, but it didn't turn out well for me. I felt this push was my last chance to do something decent with my life and start supporting myself. I should've known better; poetry is the redheaded stepchild of the art world. I just thought I had tried everything imaginable to support myself, with no luck. Other things were going on in my personal & professional lives, as well, and it took me to a dark place. I tried to kill myself, feeling like I would just drag down the few who actually cared about my well-being. It took a while to get back to myself from that, & this book, for better or worse, details that journey through the darkness. I feel like it's important for people to know that everyone, including happy-go-lucky Jay Walker, can have down times. I'm hoping that the poems in this book resonate with some readers, so that they know they're not alone in their dark places. You see, that's one thing I felt in my dark place, that I was all alone in the world, with barely a handful of exceptions, whom I would just burden with my presence in the years to come. I don't want anyone else to feel that way, so I'm putting out this book, so that everyone knows my darkness. After all, you can only defeat your darkness by bringing it into the light. At this point, it seems silly to say that I hope you *enjoy* the book, but I do hope you appreciate these poems and see the beauty in their tragedy. Thanks to all for your understanding.

                Love,

                 ~ jay.

I Used To

I used to work wonders with words
I used to paint visions in minds
                lush landscapes on the canvas of thought
I used to mold mammoth monuments
        from the clay of gray matter
          carve incredible creations
        from the most stone of hearts
Brick by brick, I would erect architectural artwork to astound
                            stanzas to scrape the sky
I used to create fireworks displays to rival the galaxies
I used to create galaxies
                    with my words
I used to
      but now
          now, all I create are questions
      mostly why?
Oh, there's still plenty of glass to bend & shape
      but there's no fire in the furnace
Before the landscape can be put onto your canvas
      it must be created in mine
All the tools are there
      but there's no motivation
I am not moved to move
      except to say that
I am not moved to move
            writing about not writing
                  again
            waiting to care enough about
                something
            wanting to make the marvels
                to be   the marvel
I used to.

The Dark

Hello.
How are you?
It's been a long time
    since you've acknowledged my presence
    since you've even looked in my direction
    since you've cared to admit
                          I'm here
   but I am   here
                         here
     I am
standing in the corner
    where you put me
      I am   here
lights out all around me
     the way I like it
      I am here
festering
scheming
lying in wait
    I
      Am
         Here
     & I'm not going anywhere
          until you acknowledge me
              look at me
              see me
              know me
              understand me
              understand why

I am here

                                    why I came
                                    why I stay
                                    why I smolder

                here in the corner
                here in the dark
                    growing darker
                becoming darker
                becoming
                        the dark
       I am   the dark
I am the black smoke billowing
   the chemical fire burning
   the cancer building
   the wounded animal bellowing shrieks of pain
        & I'm not going anywhere
           until you hear me
                see me
                feel me
                smell me
                taste me
                            in the back of your throat
          until you acknowledge me
          until you admit
       I am here
             inside you
           a part of you
         coming from you
  reaching out to destroy everything you love
        until you acknowledge me
            acknowledge
              the dark
             inside you
  stirring the dark inside others

				poking everything with sticks & stones
				never letting it rest
				never letting you rest
								until you acknowledge me
												see me
												feel me
												know me
												understand me
																love me
Love me like I've never been truly loved before
Love me
				I've never been truly loved before
				this beast, always ugly
								never understood
You clearly see the prince underneath
				& you still deny me
								turn away
								run away screaming at the beast
										abandoning the prince
										leaving him cursed
										leaving me alone in
											the dark
										growing darker
										becoming darker
										becoming
											the dark
				& then you have the nerve to wonder
								why I'm always
										so
											angry
It's because
				I'm always
				here
										alone

                        in the dark
                until you
                                        love me
            like I've never been loved before
Only then will I heal
Only then
        will I leave.

Broken Kingdom

If you were to ask
    I couldn't say that I don't still love you
        paler
      tamer
        easier substitute that
            I only realized well afterward that you are
      there were still qualities that were uniquely you
A rose by any other name would not smell quite as sweet
    as the fragrance your bloom put forth
        but your vines climbed my walls
            & tried to force your blooms everywhere
              tried to make me your kind of beautiful
        & all they did was leech off my minerals
            & bring my castle crumbling to the ground
This man who would be king
    turned peasant
        lamed by falling structure
Your flowers fed
Your pollen spread
    you bloom elsewhere
        while I lay broken
            & deep in a muck so thick
                that not even a lotus will bloom.

Only Pieces

I'd like to be friends
    with your finger
        but not your middle finger
            because that can be insulting
        & not your index
            because that can point out my flaws
        & not your ring finger
            because that's too much of a commitment
        & the thumb can be too fickle
            with its ups & downs
                    & how it can hitch a ride
                    elsewhere
      so not that one, either
I'd like to be friends with your pinky
I'd like a hug from your arms
    but that requires them to bend
      which requires the elbows
    & holding your elbows in my heart
        always seems like I'm catching them in the ribs
    so I don't want to be friends with your elbows
Can you hug me without your elbows?
                      We'll work on it
I'd love to get close to that mouth
    if you could do something about the teeth
        because I'm afraid of how they can bite
    so I don't want to be friends with your teeth
        just your lips & tongue
                like a blowjob!
    & speaking of sex
That ass is a thing of beauty
    but I don't want to be friends with the sphincter
        because I'm tired of its shit
    so I only want the glutes, please
I'd love your shoulder to cry on
    but I hate when it gets cold

And I like your liver
    but it can't handle its liquor
And your spleen seems nice
    but I'm not really sure what it does
Hmm
How silly it seems
    to only want to be friends with pieces of you
    to pack up & move out of your house
        just because you blew a fuse
    to not want to help you fix the problem
        leave you fumbling around in the dark alone
        not see where I left too much plugged in &
                turned on
        where I may have brought on this darkness
How silly to blame the house's faulty wiring
    when all flaws were fully advertised beforehand
      to abandon the whole structure
      including all the parts we built together
How silly to think I can take the finger of my choice
    & leave the rest of the hand behind
      to think I can deny
        the parts where the sun doesn't shine
      to think it possible that I could be friends
      with only the pieces of you I like
Isn't that silly?

After .CS.

The hearth is dismantled
The sky has fallen
The destinations are closed,
    & the storm has moved to other shores.
I am not fire but ash,
    not constellation but black hole upon black hole,
    not wanderlust but simply lost,
    neither chaos nor calm but simply a mess of emptiness,
                  simply cluttered with nothing.

I am but a shell with no explosive,
    a ghost with a name,
    a contradiction of self
I am & am not.
There is no more.

Jason 2000

Good evening.
My name is Jason 2000
       the Jovial
            Automaton
            Suppressing
            Offensive
            Negativity
I am programmed for the pleasure of all,
       totally devoid of all unhappy emotions
Other names were considered, but
       Happybot 2000 just seemed too
                                  campy.
I am very skilled in the areas of
       humor:
            A quadriplegic walks into a bar;
            the bartender says,
                "How'd you do that?"
       encouragement:
            Call yourself "flower" & never ever stop growing
       validation:
            You are right, dear; let's do it your way
       & sexual performance …
            but I cannot demonstrate that here.
I am insightful
   inspiring
   entertaining
   engaging, & always
   happy
        I am always
  happy
            so that you may always be happy
                because I am an android
                      not a person
                & your happiness is far more important

    [*fuckers*]
I cannot have any emotion that could be considered negative
    [*bitch*]
I am not permitted to have an opinion
  that does not compliment your own [*idiot*]
  I am incapable of feeling pain [*asshole*]
      frustration [*hypocrite*]
      disappointment [*stupid*]
      anger [*fuck you*]
      or grief [***WHY?***]
I am not allowed to be unhappy.
Ever.
For any reason.
Because that would be offensive to you
  & your happiness is far more important than mine ...
            fuckers.

Heaven forbid that I cry
  or rage
  or sigh
  or even look slightly downward
    shift my weight
    hunch my shoulders
  or make the slightest sound or emotion
that would indicate ennui
    disappointment
    sadness
    frustration
    anger
    grief
    loneliness
Heaven forbid that I do anything other than
  shuck 'n jive fo' ya', massa!
Heaven forbid I speak anything but flowers & backslapping
Heaven forbid I have opinions that are my own
Heaven forbid I don't just shut up & fuck you ... softly
          or hard

						or kinky
			because your pleasure is all I'm good for
Heaven forbid I be tired
				or sick
				or sick & tired
				so sick & tired
		of all the backstabbing
				trash-talking
					judgmental hypocrites in the world
		of not being able to count on anyone
		of hemorrhaging friends from every cut they make
				because no one can stand to be around any Jay
				but "happy-go-lucky" Jay
Heaven forbid my personality have more colors & sides
		than a Rubik's cube
				my brain to be more complex than an abacus
			never mind a computer
Heaven forbid I ever dare to even *have* pain
					never mind *show* pain
			because no matter how nicely I say it
					or how right I am to feel it
			my unhappiness is offensive to you
					& your happiness is far more important
Heaven forbid I be **_fucking human!_**
						[click]

My apologies.
There must be a glitch in my programming.
Perhaps I have come down with a virus.
		Ha. See? Humor.
I will return to the lab for re-re-re-repairs &
		r-r-rep-p-programm-mingingngngng.
						[click]
Perhaps they will have better luck
					[*go to*]
		with the next model.
					hell.

This Bone

Trying to call my muse
Silence
    but her stare barks,
        "I am not a dog"
She won't come when called
    but she'll sit
        stay
          beg me to finish what I started
            before starting more
                until I fetch my notebook from my room
                  where I left it
There, my bowl is full
Here, it lay empty
    & I'm left chasing my tale
"Bitch," I growl
    so she threw me this bone.

"Victim" Shirt

I don't like the way you wear that shirt
    all inside out
        so you can see the word "VICTIM" in your reflection
Part of me wants to tell you to take it off
        remind you that you gave it to me
                forced it on me
            then tore it off me
            took it from me
I only dressed you in the finest robes
    to match the crown I placed on your head
But you got me this threadbare print T
    shoved it on my frame & then
    ripped it off almost as quickly
        claiming it as your own
        leaving me naked in the cold wind
But part of me wants to say you're right
You *should* take the shirt
    wear the shirt
    own the shirt, since you
    made the shirt
      it's *your* shirt
You did this, so
You own this
You think you deserve better?
        deserve more?
Then you should've spent more
        invested more
        done more
        done better
Part of me wants to yell & scream
    I'm the one who *you* thought wasn't good enough
        for more than this shirt
      that's why you got it for me
        like the hundreds of others who
            got it for me
        like the hundreds of others who
            took it from me

>   like the hundreds of others who
>   keep it on me by
>   taking it from me &
>   wearing it inside out

But part of me wants to say you're right
You're *not* good enough for more than this shirt
    because that's what you put into it
You reap what you sow
    so wear what you've sewn
Keep it turned inside out, if you want
    so it says "VICTIM" in the mirror
        just so long as *I* know you got it
            backwards
Everyone knows
    I never really liked clothing anyway.

Don't

We promised we'd never let each other fall
Then, you dropped me & walked away
     as I hit the ground hard
So don't be surprised
     that the promises I kept in my pocket
         broke upon impact right along with me
& don't be offended
     that my opinion of you lays on the ground next to me
& don't be ungrateful
     when I pick up all the pieces
         & want to reconstruct a friendship
don't slap the pieces out of my hand
     & expect them to not hit the ground again
            or break even more upon new impact
don't expect me to pick them up again
don't expect me to care
         to mourn
            to stand there looking at the pieces
don't think that these pieces sit any higher
     than the ground level
         on the stairs of my many heartbreaks
don't think about it at all
don't think about *me* at all
Oh, you don't?
Good.

It'd Be Nicer

It's nice to hear the words
It'd be nicer to see them
              feel them
              believe them
It'd be nicer if there weren't always an excuse
      every time you hurt me
It'd be nicer if there were ever an apology
      every time you hurt me
It'd be nicer if there weren't an
      every time you hurt me
It'd be nicer if we could be
     nicer than just
     nice
         if I could be
     nice
         if I could not cringe inside
   every time we're in the same room
      if I could not flash back
   to the time you took advantage of me
   every time we're in the same room
      if I could not flash back
   to your hurtful words on the screen
   every time we're in the same room
 or every time I ever even think of you
It'd be nicer
        if I could be
              healed
              whole
              happy without your apology
    but it hasn't happened
       it's so hard

      it's Hell to hold on
    but it's glued to my hands
      its Hellfire heat fused it to flesh
     it's a part of me now
Medical professionals are needed
   to help me remove it
     without the salve of a sincere "I'm sorry",
      no additives
They're working
We're working
I'm working on it
Until then
   nice needs to suffice.

Fallout

There is no poetry left for you
No sunflowers grow in the soil,
       poisoned by the nuclear fallout
              from the explosion of what we had
No life swims in these polluted waters
       where we once stood on its shores admiring swans
There is no fire in the hearth of our home
There is no home
       for you demolished & abandoned it long ago
              dropped your bombs & ran away
You didn't even stay long enough
       to see the blast engulf & destroy in a day
              what took us months to build together
       blocking any & all exposure to the fallout you created
Now, all that remains is the radioactive rubble
       putting off a toxic energy that'll take a half-life-time to dissipate
The land of my heart expels this toxicity with words like
       liar
       coward
       hypocrite
       fraud
              & other words far too vulgar to repeat
There is toxicity
There is vulgarity
There is a lot of negativity
       but there is no poetry left for you
This piece
This is not for you
This is to vent
       to expel
       to release the negativity from my heart
       to heal from the damage you did
       to make this land suitable for life someday
There is no poetry left for you
This piece
       is for me.

Lake Inspiration

This great lake was deep
    & a river ran through it
        bringing fresh water to its depths
When I looked into it
    I could see my reflection clearly
When I swam it
    I was cooled
When I fished its depths for sustenance
    I was never disappointed
The abundance
The variety
The flavors that filled my senses
Like Jesus, I spread my catch
    to share with anyone & everyone who would take it
I fed dozens, maybe hundreds
    which, in turn, fed me again
Tears of pain
Tears of joy
Tears of catharsis flowed
    falling from passing clouds
        another source for the great lake
But the harsh sun shone to bright too long
    & the river's source was dammed up
The blazing heat dried up the great lake
    until it was barely a puddle
Now, when I look into it
    the water is murky
    the reflection is muddled
Now, when I want to immerse myself
    there's hardly room to dip my toes
Now, when I fish for sustenance
    I pull up only the same old line
When will the clouds form?
When will the rain fall?
When will the dam break?
I can't feed anyone like this

I can't feed myself
       & I'm starving!
Now, I'm begging in the streets for my next meal
"Feed me," I cry, "Please feed me!"
      but no one can help me
           & my heat just adds to the problem
The people demand new flavors
           new colors
           new textures
     but all I do is complain about the state of the lake
         seeing nothing in its reflection
         finding nothing in its shallowness but my line
Nothing will come by wishing
      so I'm swimming &
         fishing &
         being elsewhere for now
      but I still wish
          hope
           pray for another source to show itself
                     to bring fresh water
                     to feed my lake

I still visit
 still gaze
 still cast in hopes of finding something new to share
      trusting beyond trust
          in the natural order
The dam will break
The rain will fall
The lake will return
             eventually
             in its own time
       but sitting & waiting for it won't make it come any faster
         so I'm swimming &
           fishing &
           being elsewhere for now
           hoping I can connect these sources
                 back to my lake

                feed it from them
             make them *all* stronger
                        clearer
                        deeper
                              more abundant
hoping I can help us all feed again.

The Thing about Assholes

The thing about assholes
                            (regardless of astrology)
    is that they're assholes
They're not eyes or ears
        not hands or feet
        not noses or mouths
            they're assholes
Assholes are in the business of shit
    & business is always good
Some assholes hold onto their shit
    while some let the shit fly
Some assholes hold onto their shit too long
      'til it's hard as stone
        & hurts to get it out
Some assholes leak shit left & right
              little by little
    trying to hold on
    but the shit is too full of liquid
        & slips past shrunken sphincters
Some assholes have no shame or tact
        spew their shit all over the place
    splishy or squishy soft or stone
        come at you hard & fast
            or slow & painful
                    for everyone
    & they don't care about the mess they make
            or who they mess up
            who they hit
            who they hurt
That's what assholes do
            shit
        hold onto shit
        leak out shit
        let go of shit
        assholes ...   shit
If assholes were eyes
    they could see the mess they make

          & maybe regret it
If assholes were ears
    they could finally listen to people
        instead of always spewing their shit
    they could see & hear that the people around them
        aren't more assholes spewing shit
            but hands cleaning the mess
                hands grabbing shovels
                    hands showing them the shit they leave
                hands trying to dig us *all* out
If assholes were feet
    they could walk the talk
            live the shit they're dropping
          try to not step in it
          not get in it
          not get caught up in it
          not get in it too deep
If assholes were noses
    they could smell their own shit
            smell it stinking no better than anyone's
            smell it on themselves
       & know they're not as clean as they think
      if they can even think
                          so full of shit
          but they *can't* think
              don't think
              won't think

They're not brains
    not noses
    not feet or
        hands or
        ears or
        eyes
        they're assholes
            & assholes shit
That's what assholes do
They don't think

They don't listen
They don't walk their talk
They don't smell
    don't see the mess they make
    don't speak real
    don't speak
    don't say they're sorry
        assholes shit
It's up to us
        as whole people
    to clean up ourselves
    to not worry about messy assholes
    to leave them where they belong
                      behind.

South of the Border

There is a difference between cases & comrades
                              counselees & confidants
                            clients & kindred
    a distance that separates them from each other
        & from you
    a distinction you need to make
      line you need to draw
      border you need to patrol
              to guard
              to wall up
                  in order to protect yourself
I understand
    but I thought I had all the right paperwork
              an updated passport
          a proper visa
    I thought I alone could claim dual citizenship
    I thought that's what you told me
    I thought that's what you wrote on papers you gave me
        testimonies & testaments
        declarations of independence
             of vulnerability
              of everything inside you
          your official signature
                    at the bottom of them all
I thought I alone could cross that line
But you don't yet rule the land of casework
    & the governing body is making life stressful for you
    & too many friends are blatantly bum-rushing the border
            in broad daylight
                not sneaking under the cloak of night
Now it's too much
Now you must protect yourself
Now you let no one cross
    not even me
I've been banned from the land of clients & counselees
    & criminalized in the country of comrades & confidants
        my status set back to second-class citizen

                    sent away to suffer in the slums
              already convicted
                    waiting too long to receive my sentence
But I object to how you're using the evidence
     & will not abide this gag order
I'm filing this appeal on the grounds
     that I love you
           needed you
              hoped you would grandfather me in
                          grant me immunity
                          give me a reprieve
              from the new laws against border crossing
I felt like an Old Man with No Country
     left adrift in Open Water with no boat
           during a Perfect Storm
     Alone In The Dark again
           welcoming The End
              that never came
Fate washed me ashore in this limbo of your love
     waiting for word on my status
Will I again be granted full, dual citizenship
     or am I a second-class friend for life
           & should I consider just giving up my claim on your land
                 & sail away to other shores?

Silence

Listen; can you hear it?
Listen; it is there.
Shh! Can you feel it
All around you in the air?

... silence ...

I can hear it in the air;
I can feel it on my skin.
It seeps into my bones,
Into my soul within.

... Silence ...

It is all around me,
Above, below, before, behind.
I can't take it anymore!
It's driving me out of my mind!

... SILENCE ...

I'm going crazy!
Somebody scream!!
Somebody tell me
It's all just a dream!!!

... SILENCE ...

I cannot take anymore!
I have lost any sense of reason!
My sanity has left me alone to deal with this nightmare!
Somebody rescue me from my self!
I cannot do it on my own!
I cannot stop it; I cannot live with it,
This maddening, deafening
... silence ...

How I Could've Loved You

Sometimes, no matter where I am
    I still look at places
        at parks & parking lots
        at forests & open fields
        at beaches & back alleys, and think
          'There's a good spot for us to hang out unseen.'
It makes me think about that petite frame of yours
    with smooth, pale skin
        small, perky breasts
It reminds me of your doe eyes
    and your sweet, young, goofy smile
Girl, you sure did *look* innocent;
    maybe that's what I liked most about you
Maybe I fell for your innocent looks
    the way most women fall for my charms
        despite the fact that I tell them I'm no good
Maybe I saw in you what others see in me
    a partial wisdom beyond my years
    an apparent hardness, a strength of will
        but beneath it all is still a child that wants
                needs
                begs to be
                    loved
      and you can see that child
          through window-like eyes
Hell, maybe I could just tell that you wanted me, too;
    that always turns me on
Sometimes, I wonder why we got started
    only to end up the way we did
Sometimes, I wonder what you think of me
    if you do
        wonder what we would've said
        had our attempts at one final connection before I left
           been more fruitful

I wonder how you could say
        you cared for me & my happiness so much
                and then just discard me
                        disregard me
                              consider me 'not worth your time'
Sometimes, it hurts a little
Sometimes, it makes me think I could've loved you
        little girl that you are
    not enough to make things last
        but enough to truly say I did
Sometimes, I think I did
Sometimes, I wonder why
        wonder what I saw in someone who, in many ways
   is still a little girl, despite everything she's been through
     or maybe because of it
    wonder how I let you get such power over me
  that you destroyed me the first time
    you tried to walk away
    wonder when you decided to disregard me
  a second time
              what triggered it
              what did I do
     wonder why I cared so much
        why I care   so much
    wonder where you get off judging me like that
    wonder where I get the strength
  to not cry about it anymore
        how I make it look
          make it feel
                        so easy?
        how it can be   so easy
  if I truly loved you?
Sometimes, I wonder how I could've *loved* you, &
Sometimes, I wonder *how* I could've loved you, &
Sometimes, I wonder how I could've loved *you*.

All I Can Write About

I want to touch you, but I can't feel my hands
        frostbitten ice-block digits
                with waters shallow & still in my veins
I want to talk with you, but I lost my voice
        ghost of a whisper
                inaudible even to dogs
I'm striving to reach you, but I've lost my way
                                my sense of direction
        a compass who can't find north
Using MapQuest is hard enough *with* all the info
        but I have no starting point
                I know where I want to be
                        but not where I'm coming from
I want to open up, but I can't find the door
        the converse of the lights being on with no one home
I'm here, but I can't see me
        never mind my surroundings
Are my lights out
        or have I gone blind?
No sight
No voice
No Helen Keller references, please
        I can still *hear* my footsteps echo
                in the empty halls of my soul
I want to write poetry again
                poetry from the depths of my heart-shaped box
        wrap it up in pretty words for you
        deliver it over the microphone
        but I don't have the gift anymore
            took it back to the store for a refund
                but the money back wasn't worth it

When I write
        I want to put a little part of me in every line
                but all I can write about
                        is how I don't know who I am anymore.

The Ring

<u>I: Passing Through</u>

I drive through the town with your name
        on my journey to my new lover
I drive *through* the town with your name
        making sure to not stop
           buying fuel & disposing of waste
                at the stop before
                or the stop after
        because I'll be *damned*
           if I have to stop in *your* town
                on my way to *her*
I'll hold it
No, I'll literally hold it
        driving onehanded &
Dammit, I'll tie it in a knot, if I have to
        just so I don't have to give anything to you
                or take anything from you
           because I've given enough
                given enough time
            three-plus years of my life
                  that I can't get back
            given enough money
        rent
        utilities
        groceries
        toiletries
        accessories
        luxuries & other
        absurdities
        fuel & repair on a car that wasn't mine
            & a ring you probably sold by now
        given enough sex

despite what your liquor
                your genes
                your guilt
            will let you remember
        given enough faith
                enough encouragement
                enough love
so much that I had none left for myself
 I've given enough &
        taken enough
                enough of the blame
for your personal vices
    your lapses in memory
    your dwindling funds
& the other inconveniences you suffered
        taken enough of your excuses
for losing jobs
    hiding drinks
    missing opportunities
  & not following your dreams or
            living to your potential
        taken enough of your hypocrisy
not taking responsibility for your actions
                            your addictions
    not taking *my* excuses
            for my lack of income
                    of security
                    of realized visions
    not taking my advice
            my side
            my feelings into account
I have the safety of my child to consider
    & I won't give an inch on that

No, I've given enough
    & taken enough
    & I'd had enough, so
      I had to go, &
                    with all I had to go through
              having to go through you to get to her
                    just doesn't sit right with me
Yeah, I know it's not really you
          not really named for you
          not really your full name
    but it's the symbolism of the thing

<u>II: At First</u>

When my friend first told me about you
        I'll admit I took it with a grain of salt
                partly wanting to still sample all sorts of seasoning
                partly nursing blown-out taste buds
                        wanting life a little bland
When we first met online & talked on the phone
        I'll admit I wasn't taking it too seriously
                one hand on my cock, pumping seed out
                one hand on my mouth, holding laughs in
                        with no hands left to hold my heart
When I first met you in person, though
        everything changed
                & I knew your online pictures didn't do you justice
                & I knew you were truly magickal
                & I knew you were all the flavor I would ever need
                I knew I just had to taste you
                I knew it was serious
                 knew it was
                                          love
What I didn't know
        was how difficult the road ahead would be

III: Part of Me

It's a long drive between true love & divine Providence
  but I told myself it was worth it
    told myself it wasn't that bad
    told myself whatever it took to
    talk myself into the drive &
    talk myself into the love
  but I wasn't ready for it
    & neither was my car
The price of fuel alone was getting too close to $5 for comfort
  & there was another part of me
    that was already uncomfortable
      a part small but strong
          too strong to hold down
      a part of me felt it was too much
          too soon
      a part of me felt unsure of this
          of us
          of me
      a part of me felt unready
Now, I know they say
  that it's when you're not looking that it comes &
 I know they say
  that no one's ever *truly* ready
  that no one can ever *truly* be ready, but
    I say
  that there's such a thing as ready enough
     & a part of me just wasn't
It didn't even want to stick a toe in
  never mind take the big jump I was taking
    make the long drive I was making
As I was driving full-speed into love
     a part was looking for an off-ramp
I just didn't know one was coming so soon

<u>IV: Giant</u>

Maybe my name should be Jack
    because I found a way to reach heaven
        & it's a long, arduous climb
    but I've found a love golden & giving
        & every time I visited
            I brought a little of the gold home
                in my heart
The lovely bird who gave the gold
    was the prisoner of a giant cold & cruel
She is slowly but surely breaking free &
            remembering how to fly
    but he was not ready to let her go
Now, here's where the story changes:
I could not bring the lovely bird home
    so I had to keep climbing up & down
        bringing bits of gold to cherish until spent
The giant had spent all his gold
    & the bird would yield no more for him
        but he would not let her give any to anyone else
Taller than I
Broader than I
Tougher than I
    & with three unbreakable weapons in his ties to her
        I could not stand against him
    & it was he with his weapons
        who brought the stalk down
            ripped it from the ground
            robbed me of my gold
            kept me from my heaven
Maybe my name shouldn't be Jack, after all.

<u>V: Promises</u>

Not by letter
Not by email
Not by phone
I made a promise
      so now I must make the drive
           because you couldn't make a stand
The largest & most important parts of your life
                      your identity
                      your reason for being
    & he wanted to cut me off
        drawing lines on a paper like
            lines in the sand
        daring me to cross
    so he'd have a reason
        an excuse
        a justification for his behavior
    & I wouldn't dare cross
        more out of respect for natural boundaries
      or out of fear for
             what would happen to you
            than any wrath I might incur
So, instead of stepping forward
    stepping up
    standing up
  I stood back
    stepped aside
  letting you stand up for me
      stand up for yourself
          for your kids
          for what's right
  assuming that you would
        could
    stand up to him

                        to them
            while standing alone
                    & you couldn't
                        you couldn't risk angering
                                            alienating
                                                losing your children
                            like you could risk losing me
                                    did risk losing me
                                    did   lose me
You couldn't keep your promise
        so I had to keep mine
Not by letter
Not by email
Not by phone
            & the drive never felt so long
                    as it does today

VI: Through Again (or The Source)

I drive through the town with your name
      on my journey to my new lover
      on my journey to making her my old lover
            making her just another ex
            making her just like you
At least this one feels bad for what she did
      or didn't do
At least this one feels less like just another failure
      less like it
        but not *un*like it
              just another failure
     because I failed her
        just as much as she failed me
          failed to trust her fully
        just as much as she failed what trust I gave her
          failed to let go of my past
        just as much as she failed to escape hers
     I failed
          again
          & again
          & again
    & I can't fail again
      can't fall again
      won't fall again
      won't feel again
      won't let myself feel again
              fly again
            only to fall again
            only to fail again
            only
The drive back is just as long as the drive up
    & the drive up was never as long as it was this time
I have to stop

  to dispel waste
  to refuel
   & now there's no reason to avoid the stop in your town
As I approach the counter
  an array of colors catches my eye
Agate
  glossy, like my eyes
  stone, like my heart has become
This canister of rings calls to me
I search & quickly find what I'm looking for
  black
  black to black out this finger
   black out my heart
   black out myself
   & with this ring, I me wed
    with this ring, I symbolize my commitment
     to never letting myself down
      never letting myself fall
      never letting myself feel that pain of
       just another failure
      never letting myself feel
          again
I pull away from your town
  & feel myself pull away from everything else
   feel myself pull the door on my soul
    shut
    shutting down
    shutting down all the pain
     all the rage
     all the feeling
     into this black ring
      that I got in your town
Yeah, I know it's not really your town

& I know it's nothing more than a stone ring
but it's the symbolism of the thing

VII: Out of Symbolism

What was once a symbol of freedom
        has become a tiny shackle
What was meant to shield myself from harm
        has become a wall I can't get over
A lightweight trinket sits heavy on my hand
        black, like the cancer it has become on my heart
I don't want this rock to leave me stone cold
        when a fire still burns inside me
I don't want to black out my finger
          black out my heart
          black out the sun inside me
      eclipsing the light in my eyes
I'm not saying I'm ready for something real
I'm not saying I'm healed enough to stand
            never mind walk
I'm not saying I want love again now
I'm just saying I want love again
                       someday
      saying I want to stay open to love
              to learning
              to life
      saying I want to stay positive
           be positive
           come from positivity
        I want this to be about positive things, like
    self-love
    self-growth
    self-sufficiency
Not self-imprisonment
    self-exile
It's self-defeating
    self-serving
    self-sabotage
It's sealing out air for fear of flies

    fasting for fear of food poisoning
      denying who I am for fear of who I've been
                      who I could become again
It's foolish fallacy
    pure folly
        this false freedom I feign
I want to truly be free
              free from fear
              from falsehood
              from all that holds me down
                      holds me back
              free from the façade on my finger
    but I'm still afraid
        I'm afraid that taking off the ring
              won't take off the spell
                    the meaning
                    the magic
There's too much magic in this ring
  I put too much magic in this ring
      too much stock
      too much power
      too much symbolism
              in this ring
There was no ritual to putting it on
    but I'm too afraid to just take it off
        without some symbolic ceremony
Symbolism got me into this
I'm hoping symbolism will get me out
    then, maybe
I'm hoping I'll get out of symbolism.

VIII: The Mask

You're still here
You're gone, but
      you're still here
I can feel you
    feel you where you used to lay
        on my hand
        in my head
        on my heart
           heavy
                      making me hunch over &
                      I have a hunch
                              this isn't over

I removed you
 broke you
 washed myself clean of you
                of your energy
                of your stain on my soul
     but I didn't
        couldn't
        wasn't equipped with correct chemicals
            the black light showing the spots where
                I missed you
I sometimes find myself playing with your memory
                      twirling it around on my hand
                            in my head
                              in my heart
                  knowing you're not there, but
                  reaching for you anyway
        the weight of you pressing on me
                holding me in place
                holding me here
            chained to this spot
                  this pain tearing at me

                    this damaged child
                obsessing
                being compelled
                peeling at emotional scabs like wallpaper
                        slowly & one at a time
                making the rounds
                        so that each one gets
                                        its due attention
                        so that each one
                                never completely heals
& no one can tell
  no one can tell, because
  no one can see past the wall
                the wall that was supposed to
        come down when you came off
                                        supposed to
            crumble as you were crushed
                            pounded to dust
                            blown to the wind
                    the wall that you represented
                    the wall that is
                                still here

& no one can tell, because
        when you came off,
                the mask went on.

Gina Lee

Tommy & Gina got halfway there
    But they couldn't make it to the end
'Cuz Gina started thinking she could not share
    Her dreams or tears with her best friend
        Kept them to herself instead
        No more crying in the bed
But dreams can die, if they're not let out
    They can drown on unshed tears
Their water-logged corpses give weight to doubt
    And sink a love that's been afloat for years
        There was nothing he could do
        She never told him; he never knew
    As things slowly fell apart
    A song was building in Tommy's heart
Gina Lee
We could've made it, if you had just believed
If you would've just had faith in you & me
In the love we shared & all we planned to be,
But you never did believe
The money Gina made working hard
    Waiting tables at the diner all day,
She took it at night to the local bar
    And drank all her fears & troubles away
        Tried to wash them from her head
        But only made them worse instead
At closing time, she was too far gone
    From all the liquor that overflowed
She needed strangers to help her along,
    When home was just two blocks up the road
        Tommy tucked her into bed
        And wondered what was in her head
    In his heart, the song still grew,
    Fed on the fear of all he never knew

Gina Lee
We could've made it, if you had just believed,
If you would've just had faith in you & me
In the love we shared & all we planned to be,
But you never did believe
Finally, the time came around
    When he couldn't take any more
Tommy said, "You gotta put the bottle down
    Or I'm walking out the door."
        She'd pretend to comply
        But she'd grown to rely
        On the whiskey & rye
        But she was living a lie
        And couldn't understand why
        Tommy Jay said, "Goodbye."
Now, it's been a few years since the end
    Of Gina Lee & Tommy Jay
They couldn't even stay each other's friend
    Maybe they're both better off that way
        Within reach but out of touch
        That kind of pain is just too much
        There ain't no living on unanswered prayers
        But in Tommy's heart, the wound's still there
        No, the love is gone, but there's still the song
        And it heals his heart, when he sings it strong
Gina Lee
We could've made it, if you had just believed,
If you would've just had faith in you & me,
In the love we shared & all we planned to be,
But you never did believe, did you?
Gina Lee
Our love could've lasted through eternity
If only you had deemed yourself worthy
Believed in yourself & in all that you could be,
But you never did believe.

Fragments

My brain is leaking
    a little bit at a time
        grey matter eking out
  drop by drop
      grey matter forming
          on this college-lined & hole-punched paper towel
      grey droplets collecting
        in splotches all over
here & there
        every design painting a different picture
            telling a different story
      in pieces & fragments
          fragments never meeting
              never connecting
              never finishing
Inspiration bullets hit me
        open me
         tap me to leak grey sap
   sticking graphite grey to these pages
      but never to me
        never before time
          before pressure
          before obligation closes my reservoirs
              stops my flow
                  & flows away
   leaving leaked brain fragments forever fractured
              never finished
            never connected
I want to take scalpel & saw on myself
        open wide a single flood gate
        unhinge my head &
        let the grey matter spill
        let it loose upon leaves
        let splotches collect & connect
    creating canvasses to rival Rorschach
              to please Pollack & Picasso
    creating canvasses complete

                        complete for copying
            to hang on your walls
            to give you pieces of me
                        pictures of me
                                complete
                        pictures of a
                                complete me
            to   complete me
But the world keeps spinning
    mirrored by gears moving
                hands moving to
                numbers moving
        the world   moving
                    us all
            & these fragments sit soaked into the page
                    fragments forever
                                    unfinished.

This Is Alone

This is more than just the piece not fitting in place
This is the piece being the wrong size
                              color
                              shape
    to go anywhere in the whole puzzle
This is more than just the sprinter in a marathon
This is the sprinter in the biathlon
     the figure skater power-lifting
     the Jamaican bobsled team
This is more than just an ugly duckling
This is the duckling growing up to find
    he's a platypus
               not even the right species
           & doesn't know how to fit in either world
This is more than just lost in the wilderness
This is lost in the bad parts of the big city
    with all the wrong maps
        a faulty GPS
        a broken compass
    & at every stop
          no one speaks your language
This is more than just lonely
This is Red Dwarf with no cat
                  no android
                       no hologram or computer
This is trimethylaminuria
    never smelling your own fishy odor
    showering every day & never being clean
This is the unicorn on the shrinking island
    staring at the ark, as it sails away
This is alone.

Four-Letter Word

Hope is a four-letter word
    a curse word
        something left for those with limited vocabulary
    & I have learned too many words
        in the School of Hard Knocks
I am the Webster of woe
    the Roget of regret
    the encyclopedia of ennui
    the champion of Scrabble: Sorrow Edition
        the point is
Hope is a four-letter word
    a curse word
    a curse on all who hear it
    a hex
    like voodoo
        turning folks into zombies
        infecting them with this disease
        affecting how they see the world
            finding intangible hope
                hidden in all the very real pain
    & I have learned too many words
        in the School of Hard Knocks
My vocabulary is too broad
    to resort to four-letter words
        like hope
    I have learned too many lessons
        to believe in a thing like hope
A unicorn of concepts
The only place to find it in my world
    is in dictionaries
        & books of fantasy
A tooth fairy leaving nothing but promises under pillows
    & I've lost all my baby teeth chewing on its lies

I deal only with facts
    & the fact is
        in the end
    everything ends
    everything leaves
    everything dies
        in the end
      it's the end
Nothing is forever
    so how can there be any such thing
      as hope?
  intangible
  imaginary
  deceitful
  foul
  vulgar
  accursed
      four-letter word.

I, Picasso

You can turn on the lights
    but you can't repaint the canvas
        & still call the picture mine
    & you haven't yet been able to teach me
        how to repaint it myself
        how to use different colors
                lines
                shading
        how to have different focal points
            different subjects
            different views
You can't remove my eyes
    or detach them from my heart
No *prescription* has ever helped me see any better
No *contact* has ever cleared my vision
No one has ever changed what I see
I have been given the tools, but
        try as I might
    I am forever in a blue period
        painting different angles of Guernica.

Like Forever

You feel like forever
    but I've never been good at telling time
        with other people's clocks
    so used to being guided by stars, moons, & planets
        I can't adjust to that brand of nuclear power
          can't read that kind of satellite
You feel like forever
    but I haven't been able to trust my senses for awhile
        things looking
            sounding, even
              tasting like forever on my tongue
        but eventually becoming ugly
                  discordant
                  poisonous still
    but you still feel like forever
          like nothing ever before
          like little bits of everything before
      the promises of yesterday
        echoing into tomorrow &
            tomorrow &
            tomorrow
  until there is no more tomorrow
but no senses can reach that far away
I'm having trouble picking up those sounds from
                  that far away
    just as I feel your words putting more distance between us
        the connection growing more & more static
                  stretched
                  stagnant
      like pools of salt water
        sitting waiting behind my eyes
      I am sitting waiting behind my eyes
          waiting for my forever
        waiting   forever
            but forever
     feels so far away

The further away I go
The further away you grow
    until I can't feel you
     & I want to feel you
          feel you with me
   even when you're not with me
But the more you're not with me
   the more you're not with me
    until I can't feel you
    until I   feel
          like forever
because you feel like forever
          & forever
          feels so far away.

Fueling the Fire

The same fire that keeps the wolves at bay
    alerts them to your presence
The same fire that pushes away the darkness
    makes the shadows dance
The same fire that feeds off the air
    is threatened by the wind
        that heats the night
    is hindered by the cold
How do you keep the fire going, knowing this?
Where do you find the fuel?
How do you stay alight
    in a world that wants to consume you
        blind you
        freeze you through & through?
How do you keep afire in a wet
        cold
        dark
        dangerous world?
I've been searching for would
    but I can't see the forest for the trees
I've run out of gas
My wick is too burned out to catch
    & the alcohol
        is too dangerous a fuel
        makes the fire unstable
        burns more than intended
    I don't like to depend on it
So, I remain lost in the wilderness
    fire falling
      failing
        flickering to faint embers
      searching for the fuel to keep it going in this cold world
        but I am all wet
            shivering
            sore
            weak
            ready

       to let the wolves consume
          the darkness surround me
          the weather wear me down
      ready to let the fire die
I know a phoenix egg incubates in the embers
   but the fire is a double-edged sword
     & I'm afraid of pacing wolves & dancing shadows
       of going deeper into wilderness
               with no paths
      of burning myself again
       & of darkness yet to come
I haven't seen sunshine in months
I wonder if it will ever come
I wonder how long I can wait
   how long I can hold out
      hold on
   how long I can last
  lost in the wilderness
    afraid of a fire that both saves me
     & enslaves me
      indebts me to its existence
      exposes me to dangers
      torments me with shadows
      taunts me with its frailty
    afraid of a fire
       that burns
Knowing this,
   how do *you* keep the fire going?

Against My Nature

There is a war raging inside me
    between heart & mind
    between how I love & what I fear
    between how I naturally am
        & how the world has taught me to be
It's not like me to hide from the spotlight
        to run headlong & screaming
                      into the arms of obscurity
    to shy away from human contact
  but that's how I feel
        like shunning humanity
          shucking my public persona
          shunting so-called responsibilities
          shuffling into unseen corners
          shutting out the world
Body pillow bed mate beckons
    "Rest your sorrows & sob into soft blue safety;
    sleep so long, until The Long Sleep surrounds you
      & surrender."
It sounds
      so good
          just stopping the world & getting off
          just stopping the whirlwind in my mind
          just stopping the worry of worthlessness
  but I tried
   & I failed
   & I'm still here
        there must be a *reason* for that
So, I hold on
        hapless
        helpless
        hopeless
  I hold on
      waiting for my purpose to reveal itself
  I walk on
  walk every day
      for sunlight

```
                    air
                    exercise
                    alone time
        I walk every day
          see people everyday
            struggle against my nature everyday
                    simultaneously tipping my hat
                        & hiding under it
                            hoping I'm not recognized
                    longing for human contact
                        & shying away from it
                            fearing all friends turn false in time
Frail, red stain glass ornament hanging on my bone tree
        looking mosaic
                patchwork
                    piecemeal from piss-poor repair after
                                        repair after
                                        repair
                    & I have no more glue
I can't take another shattering
So, I struggle against my nature everyday
    I am      against my nature
                against my tendency to trust
                            to reach out
                            to connect
Connection just closes the circuit
                conducts the current
                cooks my convict corpse
Connection just kills me
                    every time
So, I struggle against my nature everyday
        hands of friendship attached to arms outstretched extra far
            still making connections
                            at a distance.
```

Forgetting

You forgot
You forgot about your promise
              your promise to not let me forget
You   let me forget
    how to breathe
    how to climb mountains
    how to fly
You let me forget
    how it feels to have you with me
                beside me
                inside me
        even thousands of miles away
          to have your love
              your friendship
              your support
              your promise
You forgot about your promise
    & now my soul lies comatose
        forever damaged from lack of oxygen & malnutrition
          being deprived of the sustenance of you
      my soul lies comatose
    next to our friendship
        beaten bloody & on life support
    upstairs from my dreams of forever
        sheets over their heads
        growing cold in their drawers
You forgot about your promise
    & it makes me want to forget about you
        but I can't forget
I can't forget bonding at backyard bonfires
          neighborhood strolls with fireflies dancing
          popcorn fights & old movies
          the futon, the shower, the kitchen counter
          slow dancing on a moonlit beach
          book obsessions become bookcase obsessions
          weekend getaways & weeknight poetry
          meals with my folks or with yours

     all those swans swimming or sleeping
       right there, as if I planned it
I can't forget how we loved
    how quickly
     strongly
      completely
    how we made love
    how tenderly
     passionately
     beautifully
    how we spoke love
    how truly
     deeply
     profoundly
     poetically
     permanently
     we spoke love permanently
  promising to *always* be there
     always
    whether just friends or lovers
    whether good times or bad
    whether perfect or perfectly imperfect
     always
        & you weren't
For one brief moment, you weren't there
For the sake of strangers, you weren't there
When I desperately needed you, you weren't there for me
       chose to not be there for me
      chose to judge me
       scold me
       punish me
       ignore me
       leave me
You left me
    stunned in a state of shock
   left me gasping guppy-like for gulps of air
     forgetting how to breathe

```
              forgetting why I'd want to
              forgetting what the point is
You left me
              alone
                    again
       I am alone again
              widower to a dream
              mourning on paper
              eulogizing the promise made &
                    the promise shown
                    the promise of friendship
                             faithfulness
                             forever
                                            broken
I am                                        broken
I am alone again
       wishing I could forget
              as easily as you.
```

How Do You Do It?

How do you do it?
How do you rise like the undead?
How can you even stir to that dissonant reveille
    rise & shamble through that ritual?
How do you clean your face
        put on that mask &
        stretch into that one-size-fits-all uniform?
How do you conform
        confine yourself
        constrain to fit in their box &
                box away your dreams
    to rot in cerebral attics & cardiac cellars?
How do you bury Fortunado fantasies
        wall them up, as they cough & scream
        leave them to die, in your Montresor malice
    as if they sunk serpent teeth into your sole
        before you stomped them
    as if they injured
        insulted
        instilled anything other than inspiration?
or is it more like Mozart
        timeless treasure tepidly tossed like trash
                piled into paupers' pit
        the dead outnumbering the mourners
        the site forgotten & lost over time?
How do you forget your dreams &
        find the strength to
        forge ahead
    fitting in their box
        their place
        their design
    serving sibling sheeple
    feeding fellow flock members
        fattening egos for the slaughter of us all
    heart hindered & humbled to hobby
                or less?
How do you stay in the shadows inside you

   showing only a semblance of the self in your center?
How do you stand it?
How do you stand?
How do you cope?
How do you live
    this half-life
  living but not alive
    undead shuffling
      shambling through black magic ritual
  & come home to rest in piece
    lying in wait for tomorrow's turn?
How do you do it?
Help me
  understand.

Lady Winter (or Here & Gone)

The calendar says different
    but this pavement has already been defiled
        a pale, white, heavenly orgy of flakes
        sliding silky soft sensual across tarmac skin
The calendar says different
    but I can feel Winter already seeping into my bones
                      steeping into my blood
                                                    like tea
        my heart turning earl grey
The calendar says different
    but the cold wind is a worn blanket
        frayed & ineffective
        hanging on
        clinging to
        wrapping around me straightjacket tight
    & I will dislocate my shoulder
          put myself through pain
        if it means getting out
In New England, Winter is a cruel mistress
Her warm holiday heart is foretold by her cold hands
    wrapping around throats & tender parts
    taking the breath from me
        whipping winds
        scarf gags
        feather flakes turned blindfold blizzards
Her BDSM love is tough to handle
    when the safe word is "cabin fever"
When she is here
    I am gone
        lights on but not home, or
        shades open but sleeping through life
I can't take another ice kiss
    freezing streams of thought
    frosting over windows to my soul

As much as it pains me to break the chains of family ties
                to bend
                    twist
                        stretch the bonds
                                the ties that bind my heart
                                                        here
    I must escape this cold dungeon
         before my mistress goes too far
                                & kills me
When next she is here,
    I must be gone
I already have plans perfectly laid out
    but I wasn't expecting her so early
Winter is here early
The calendar says different
    but clocks are made by human hands
Her piercing eyes can't read round or red
    all words & numbers a foreign language
            she cares not to learn
Winter is here early
I hear her voice on the wind
  feel her breath on my neck
  see her white carpet rolled out before her
        flakes falling like flower petals in front of her feet
                & I am out of time
The calendar says different
    but I know different
Winter is here early
    & I am gone.

Your Act & My Stage

Your act of prestidigitation
        is knock-off novice novelty at best
When you yanked your white linen love & support
            hard & fast from my table
      my already-pieced-back-together
                      china & stemware world
          came crashing down around me
      & I wasn't the only one booing & jeering
            as you walked off my stage
                  before I could throw you off
Now you say your act has improved
        but you tremble as you timidly tiptoe to the table
            support shaking in your hesitant hand
Your stumble & bump didn't send stemware slipping
            the way you think it did
        but my words of caution come across your sensitive ears
            as more boos & jeers
              & you're indignant
                    inconsolable
                    incorrigible
              & I won't standing-O for it!
You storm off stage again, before anything can be fixed
        but the cup of love you gave me
            was the only thing re-broken
I won't invite you back to my stage
        so I'll just throw these pieces away
Just don't try to tell me your trick worked
        just because my table's reset
It took a lot of time, effort, & resources
        to repair or replace what you broke
    & don't try to tell me you never pulled that cloth
                          from my table
                  or the wool over my eyes
        when you know you did

   & don't try to tell me you made reparations
               to help repair the last damage
Your reactions prove the check was rubber
       as fake & insecure as the cloth
                 & as its owner
But my table
             is stronger now
     & it is set with sturdier stuff
           that won't crumble in clumsy hands
Besides,
      I'm all set with carnival clowns & sideshow freaks
           & slick sleight-of-hand con artists
The stage is set now
     only for someone
          with *real* magic.

Splinters

Call me a little nuts
        but you planted something in me
                something that grew
                        & grew
                                so large
            it could not be ignored
            & I tried
                    until I stopped trying
                    until I started trying for us
    but the more I tried for us
        the more you pushed away
            until what you planted had been uprooted
                              & taken away
Now, I stand alone
        while you tend someone else's grounds
      but the hole still remains
            with splinters embedded deep in my heart skin
                    & no one with tweezers
After all these years, I just wanna know
        how do I get you out?

Wildfire

You were careless
    struck the match of goodbye
     tossed it into the overgrown brush of my pain
  & walked away
       while this fire built & raged across my landscape
Now it threatens to consume me
          destroy me
          burn away all that I am inside
    leaving a hollow husk
       a burnt-out shell
       an inner wasteland
The more it burns, the more it hurts
The more it hurts, the more it burns
This perfect trio of combustion
This fuel never ending
     feeding itself
     creating itself
This twisted dark phoenix of pain rising from its own ash
                      just to burn again

This anger
This heat building from the inside out
This empty air where you once stood
       not a vacuum
    but a cold wind fanning hot flames
Absence makes the heart grow furiouser
     makes the flames grow wilder
      & I don't know how to put it out
The waters of forgiveness don't flow through this land
    or yours, it seems
You were supposed to show me how to dowse for these waters
              how to dig a well
               how to irrigate my land
You were supposed to show me how to trim my landscape
    not set it ablaze
    not burn me down
Who are you to burn me so badly?
Who are you to judge me so harshly?

Who are you to be so careless with a heart?
Yes, I'm still angry
Why am I still angry?
Why am I still burning, after all this time?
    & how do I stop without you?
        how do I save myself from this wildfire in my soul?

Fall

Leaves fall from the trees
I need to be reminded that death can be beautiful
        because I feel ugly
                in the reflection of your eyes
They are funhouse mirrors
        distorting the truth of me
But you swear the vision is real
    you refuse to hear otherwise
No matter how straight I stand
        you will always see me as crooked
Time to leave the funhouse
        leave the carnival
        leave the friendship behind
    like leaves fall from the trees
          let it fall from my limbs
                from my grasp
                from my life
          let it fall dead on the ground
          let me see it as a good thing
I need to be reminded that I can be beautiful.

A Shakespearean Tragedy

A rose by any other name would smell as sweet
       & your sunflower still smells
              like the fertilizer you're using
Call yourself what you will;
       you're still the same hypocrite to me
Two years gone
       & you still haven't offered a flower of forgiveness
              that you expected to bloom in my heart
                      after just one midsummer
Well, I'm sorry
       but the seeds of your sorry "I'm sorry"
              were ripped out of my already damaged soil
       & if you think it's only *my* hands in that garden patch,
              well, that's part of the problem, isn't it?
The other part is your weak seed
              your dud
              your unstable
                  incomplete
              insincere "sorry",
still skittish
       worried
       wary of my fury
              my tempest temper
              but my storm could've stayed calm
                  if you truly understood your effects
                        on my climate change
I don't call the storm
       until after you banish me to my island inside
You don't have to fear the fury of feelings
       if you don't keep them caged

This shrew need not be tamed but merely loved
                                                                                   accepted
                                                                                   supported
                                                                                  validated
If your love were a more constant thing
        I could've suffered the slings & arrows
                                                            of outrageous fortune
                    rather than taking arms
                                        against the sea of my troubles
I'm not saying it's your fault I faltered in my Flower-y philosophy
I'm saying my forgiveness should've eased your fear
        & it didn't
                which portrays apologies as paltry
                                  put on
                                  posturing
I'm saying I had just cause to renew my anger
I'm saying I'm still angry
        still hurting
        still needing a real apology
    which I know I'll never get
Ay, there's the rub.

Memory Breeze Through a Wind Chime Heart

I wish I could tell you I was wrong
    to wish away the whirlwind
        when it sent me flying
I've always been afraid of falling
As you tossed me around in your love
    I didn't know how secure you held me
I sought stable soil to stand on
I didn't know that everywhere I landed
    would quake & crack my foundation
        & destroy anything I tried to build
I didn't know the real security
    was hidden in the hurricane
But hurricanes come & go
They crash into our shore
    damage the structures on the ground
    & are gone the next day
The ground dragged us apart
The ground dragged us down
The ground dragged us away
    me to the west
        you to Heaven
Your winds have died down to a memory
    that blows through my wind chime heart
        every once in a while
    broken pieces
        but oh, how they sing
The sound makes me want the whirlwind back
        makes me want to leave the ground
        makes me want to fly
Too many faults all around me
    & none lie on other lands
                allegedly
I have been made a lonely island
    deserted, where nothing grows
        & nothing can be built
    & I just want to know again

   what it's like to soar above it all
With all the rises & falls
  at least I was flying
It was everyone else's gravity
  that made me crash
Now I want to take off again
  but no wind meets my whistle
Yours was under another's wing, when you were taken
  someone with enough faith in your support
Were you here, my whistle wouldn't call you, anyway
Now you dance in Heaven
  & while others feel you there enough to lift them up
    I can only feel your breeze blow through
      the wind chime pieces of my broken heart

  but oh, how they sing.

Assorted Haiku, Senryu, & Tanka, Continued

Seasons Change
Spring love; summer heat;
Fall's "not yet" leaves a blanket
Of new Winter's "no."

                                      Black Sheep Heart
                              This black sheep needs its
                            Heart to be the shepherd it
                                Always should have been.

                                                                  Heart-ship
                                            Steering this heart-ship,
                              The throttle sometimes sticks, but
                                     The rudder stays true.

                                The Pain
                       My heart hurts so much;
                    Still, I guess it's better than
                           The alternative.

Six Degrees
Would you like to know
How all movie actors link
To Kevin Bacon?

                    No hats on the bed:
                    A silly superstition
                    That I still follow.

                                        See? I can *so* be
                                In love and still write poems
                                  About other things!

                  Don't have a disease,
              Thoughtful and caring lover,
                So what's wrong with me?

Complications
I am so in love,
But she is complicated;
I can only wait.

So Close
Once again, I come
So close to Slam victory,
Just beyond my grasp.

If great poetry
Isn't saving your life, then
You're doing it wrong.

Aspiration
I can't be with you,
But I'll always aspire to
Be worthy of you.

Those who find insult
In the truth perhaps deserve
To be insulted.

Love & Hate
I'll always love you;
That's the exact reason why
I'll always hate you.

Driving to Worcester,
A group of anxious poets
Write some more haiku.

Enough
I want but don't need
To be naked with you; just
With you is enough.

The Escape
The only way to
Escape pain is to embrace
It as part of life.

A Secret
I would tell the world,
But your "not yet" holds my tongue,
For your comfort's sake.

Deal
I'll learn to deal with
Not being your man, as long
As I'm still your boy.

Give Thanks
Dear God, I thank you
For this breath of life; right now,
it hurts, but it's mine.

You + Me
You keep doing you;
I'll keep doing me, hoping
Soon, we can do us.

My Fear
I'm afraid that I
May have to let you go to
Prove how I love you.

Jealous Mourning
I cry for old friends
Who know what it's like to miss
A beloved dad.

Let's Go
Enough of pining;
If I want to be worthy,
I have work to do.

Working
You're working on you;
The bright side: it gives me time
To do work on me.

The End?
I am wondering
If this is the end or just
A pause for this muse.

Anonymous
Anonymous means
The words were more important
Than where they came from.

Bad Math
More women than men,
Yet we're still treating them like
A minority,
Pay them less but charge them more.
It just doesn't add up ... man.

Our Love's Journey
I wrote some haiku
Detailing our love's journey;
It didn't end well.

Arts Life

Being in the arts
Is all I ever wanted
To do with my life.

A Mountain that Moved
(or Fear's Bitch)

I once compared our love to mountain climbing
    but that was when I thought the ground was sturdy
I had no idea the mountain would move
I fell from our mountain
    as you sent it crumbling under me
Now I lay
        years later
    still under the rubble
        waiting for someone to come rescue me
You've made it clear it won't be you
You're no St. Bernard to pull me from the avalanche
You're a different kind of bitch
    whatever breed turns tail & runs
        at the first sign of trouble
Fear is your master
Now I lay
        years later
    still under the rubble
    still damaged
    still hurting
    still not healed of the wounds you left
You're not willing to dress them
            address them
            address me
            talk to me
            talk it out
            talk about hypocrisy
Yes, I was damaged before you got to me
    but so were you
        & you credited me with healing you
The least you could've done
    was return the favor before leaving
        not make it worse
Now I am   worse
Now I am
    still not healed

Now I lay
         years later
    still under the rubble
      that you brought down on me
         when you pulled your support of our mountain
& I don't know how to climb out from underneath it
   don't know how to dress the wounds
          set the breaks
         heal the damage
  I don't know how to heal
                not without help
You've made it clear it won't be you
You're no Florence Nightingale
You're not the healer you pretend to be
You just play the role for everyone but those who love you
              those you claim to love
   but your love is a fickle thing
       a mountain that moves
           that crumbles
               under the slightest weight
Now I lay
       years later
   still under the rubble
   & I don't know how to climb out
   & I don't know how to heal
   & I don't know if I'll ever climb mountains again
Fear is my master
   & I its bitch.

The Ground of Us

You have always wo...rn your flaws upon your sleeve
    & I have always bu...ried them deep beneath the ground
Actually, that's backwards
I would wear my heart on my sleeves
    if I bothered with clothing
Instead, I stand exposed to the elements &
            everyone
              everywhere
Wearing my heart on my naked wrist
    would be redundant
You have your flaws buried deep beneath boatloads of bullshit
    you painted pretty & say is sunshine
But earth always turns, as the
   earth always turns
     & my jagged heart is a trowel
          for your well-fertilized garden
I dig up your sunflowers without even trying
    & reveal the stone underneath
        breaking both in the process
But a stone is a stone
        even chipped
        while you can't call an upside-down heart a spade
          if it's too broken to dig
My tools lie discarded
    while your stone finds family
         gathers moss
My mettle is metal, though
I can recycle
   renew
   retool the tool
I can melt it myself with my own phoenix heat
   re-forge it
      stronger
          so as to not crack & fall apart
              on stone disguised in fertile soil
    but that's okay
All ground has its flaws, I guess

Dig them up
Let's finish what we started
We'll never finish what we started,
      leaving unsaid seeds blocked by your stone,
           but rest assured what we started is finished;
      nothing can grow in this poisoned field
                  this scorched earth
        still with embers smoldering
The ground of us is too flawed
It's long past time I move on.

America, Noun

America
A-M-E-R-I-C-A, America
Noun
From the Italian Amerigo
    which itself is from the German Amalric or Heimrich
        meaning "work ruler" or "home ruler"
America
Noun
From the English America
    meaning conflict
        conflict with England
           with Spain
           with Mexico
           with France
           with Africa
           with natives
           with itself
America
Noun
From the American
    meaning equality
        freedom
        liberty & justice for all
            for all white male landowners
Not women
Not people of color
Not the homeless
Just white
    male
        landowners
America
Noun
From the human
    meaning change

                        change the way we think
                                the way we rule
                                the way we represent
                                the way we live
                                the way we *all* live
America
Noun
        meaning potential
                potential achievement
            potential growth
                potential to be the best possible version of you
America
        meaning
                                        the best possible version of you
America,
        where is the best possible version of you?
        when will you reach your potential?
        when will you grow?
        when will you change?
        when will you achieve liberty & justice for all?
        when will the conflict end?
        when will you stop fighting with yourself?
                                        with the world?
                                        with The Universe?
        when will you live & let live?
        when will you love thy neighbor?
        when will you realize that anyone
                        that *everyone* can be an American?
        when will you know
                        what America means?

97

About the Author

Jason E. Walker, "Jay" to friends & colleagues, was born and raised in Cranston, which is a suburb bordering the south of Rhode Island's capital city, Providence. He started writing for school projects and fell in love with the medium of poetry. In the early 90s, he discovered performance poetry and the world of Slam; he felt it was a natural fit for an actor like him. In 1999, Jay won a spot as an alternate on the Providence Poetry Slam team, just missing out on the trip to the National Poetry Slam Championships that year. In the early 2000s, Jay wrote for Providence Monthly Magazine; an article he did on winter holidays garnered the mag with a Michael P. Metcalf Award for Diversity in Media from the RI Chapter of the National Conference on Community and Justice. He's been a co-host of the Spoken Word Poetry Series and GotPoetry! Live, both on Providence's historic East Side. He has three other published collections of poetry available for purchase. In 2019, he won the Favorite Spoken Word Artist award from Motif Magazine. Currently, he lives in Hopedale, Massachusetts, but he's planning to move back to RI shortly. He's working on his first novel as we speak.

www.ingramcontent.com/pod-product-compliance
Lightning Source LLC
Chambersburg PA
CBHW060207050426
42446CB00013B/3015